THE FIGHTING PARSON

THE LIFE OF REVEREND LESLIE SPRACKLIN (CANADA'S ELIOT NESS)

ORGANIZED CRIME SERIES #2

ROSE KEEFE

Absolute Crime Press
ANAHEIM, CALIFORNIA

**ABSOLUTE
CRIME**

www.AbsoluteCrime.com

Contents

ABOUT ABSOLUTE CRIME

Absolute Crime publishes only the best true crime literature. Our focus is on the crimes that you've probably never heard of, but you are fascinated to read more about. With each engaging and gripping story, we try to let readers relive moments in history that some people have tried to forget.

Remember, our books are not meant for the faint at heart. We don't hold back--if a crime is bloody, we let the words splatter across the page so you can experience the crime in the most horrifying way!

If you enjoy this book, please visit our homepage (www.AbsoluteCrime.com) to see other books we offer; if you have any feedback, we'd love to hear from you!

Sign up for our mailing list, and we'll send you out a free true crime book!

http://www.absolutecrime.com/newsletter

Reverend J.O.L. Spracklin's team of Canadian 'Untouchables'.

INTRODUCTION

As the Prohibition movement grew throughout North America during the early 1900s, most supporters signed petitions, attended rallies, and voted for pro-temperance politicians. But a handful took their dedication one giant step further. Carrie Nation, the elderly firebrand from Kansas whose response to the assassination of President William McKinley was "All drinkers get what they deserve", smashed up saloons with her trademark hatchet. Ex-ballplayer and evangelist Billy Sunday dominated pulpits and stages with his show-stopping 'Get on the Water Wagon' sermon, and was famous for such dry slogans as "Whiskey and beer are all right in their place, but their place is in hell." His histrionic speeches drew crowds and eased the passage of Prohibition into law.

The only thing that Canada's Reverend John Oswald Leslie Spracklin had in common with

Nation or Sunday was a fanatical hatred of the liquor traffic. He was no aging zealot conducting a purity campaign. When the Attorney-General of Ontario authorized him to enforce the Ontario Temperance Act in July 1920, Spracklin was a thirty-three year old Methodist minister who still retained the athletic build that he had cultivated as a college rugby player. With the power of the provincial government behind him, the charismatic clergyman bypassed vaudevillian tactics in favor of fighting the Windsor and Detroit area bootleggers and gangsters on their own terms. Historian C.H. Gervais described Spracklin as "a kind of teetotalling Wyatt Earp, who stopped at nothing to win."[1]

The Toronto Daily Star, which had anticipated his appointment as a liquor license inspector (as Ontario Prohibition agents were called) for months, announced gleefully on July 31, 1920:

---

[1] C.H. Gervais, *The Rumrunners: a Prohibition Scrapbook.* (Scarborough: Firefly Books, 1980) p. 119

Bootlegging circles in Windsor and the Border Cities last night whispered the name of Spracklin over the wires in the same tones as did the English mother that of Black Douglas in the days of old, "Hush ye, hush ye, Spracklin will not get ye."

"Don't be so sure of that!" said Spracklin as he appeared unexpectedly in the ... roadhouses....

Reverend Spracklin was a gangster's worst nightmare. Known to the press and public as the 'Fighting Parson', he and his handpicked squad of dry agents burst into the roadhouses of Essex County with pistols drawn and fists clenched. They chased liquor-laden vehicles through dark city streets and along rough country roads, and intercepted rumrunners on the Detroit River in their high-powered speed-boat, the Panther II. The minister went, often alone, into the most dangerous nightspots of 1920s Windsor, and responded to opposition by punching, not preaching. He thought noth-ing of carrying around a stack of blank search warrants and filling them out himself as needed. He could not be scared or bought, and he survived one assassination attempt after another. It was only when a roadhouse owner who also happened to be a long-time enemy died at his hands that the campaign was finally stopped.

CHAPTER 1

John Oswald Leslie Spracklin, or 'Leslie' as his friends and family called him, was born in Woodstock, Ontario, on December 4, 1886. His father, Joseph, worked as a harness maker while his mother, Charity, tended to her growing family. In 1894, when Leslie was eight, the Spracklins moved to Windsor, the southernmost city in Canada.

Windsor had been incorporated as a city only two years previously but was growing fast, largely thanks to the whiskey business. After the Great Western Railway selected Windsor as its termination point in 1854, Canadian and American business leaders hurried to set up shop there. One of them, a grocer from Detroit named Hiram Walker, opened a distillery that produced the now-famous Canadian Club whiskey. Walker also built homes for his workers and gradually developed a company town that was aptly named 'Walker's Town'. (It was later changed to Walkerville.)

It's doubtful that the Spracklin family had many dealings in Walkerville. They were staunch Methodists, and regarded alcohol as a key factor in marital breakdown, spousal abuse, and other social ills. Most of Canada's leading temperance advocates were Methodists. During the nineteenth century, their influence was felt even in cities as large as Toronto, where alcohol sales had been strictly controlled and anyone who violated the Lord's Day Act risked serious punishment, earning the city the nickname of "Methodist Rome".[2]

Leslie Spracklin was an active boy who grew into an athletic young man. He and two of his brothers, William and Arthur, showed boxing talent at an early age: Arthur even trained with

[2] "The way we were in Toronto in 1892." Trish Worron. *Toronto Star*. Nov 1, 2002. pg. A.29

the celebrated Tommy Burns.3 Leslie also excelled as a rugby player, leading his school team to several triumphs. He ignored the bruises, black eyes, and other minor injuries incurred on the field, seeing them as a small price to pay for victory.

Although not outgoing, Spracklin got along with most people. He was well-spoken, polite, and liked by his friends. But there was one individual who was destined to be a lifelong thorn in his side: Clarence Beverly Trumble.

Spracklin and Trumble, who was nicknamed 'Babe' because of his good looks, had played together as boys back in Woodstock, but by the time they were teenagers in Windsor, the association had soured. They competed over everything: sports prizes, girls, and the esteem of their peers. The handsome and charismatic Trumble was the more popular of the two, which Spracklin resented. Their mothers, who had been childhood friends, tried to stop the feud, but to no avail. The mutual antagonism worsened when Spracklin went into the

---

[3] *Toronto Star*, July 31, 1920

Methodist ministry and Trumble took over a roadhouse, but neither could have predicted the deadly turn it was destined to take.

Although he became famous as a crusading clergyman, Spracklin originally trained as a mechanic. After a brief period of military service with the 21st Regiment, Essex Fusiliers4, he took a job at the Ford Motor Car Company, which had been established in Windsor in 1904 and employed hundreds. A worker-based community known as 'Ford City' developed around the industrial complex where the automobiles were manufactured. The booming automotive industry would gradually change Windsor from a collection of border communities (Windsor proper, Ford City, Walkerville, and Sandwich, which was also the seat of government and the courts for Essex County) into a single city with a population of over 100,000.

---

[4] Library and Archives Canada; Ottawa, Ontario, Canada; *Department of Militia and Defence, Accounts and Pay Branch, Nominal Rolls and Paylists for the Volunteer Militia, 1855-1914*; Record Group Number: *R180-100-9-E*; Volume Number: *70*.

Kathy Rappaport's grandfather, Ernest, worked with Leslie Spracklin at Ford. "My grandfather always said that Spracklin was a bit strange," she says. "He was pleasant to everyone, but not much of a socializer. When the other workers went out to the bars on payday, he never joined them unless he wanted to keep an eye on a friend. It all makes sense now, seeing how he became a Prohibition agent (sic). But some of the men thought he was stuck up. He didn't drink or swear. My grandfather said that he would tell off any man who swore in front of a lady."5

Ford mechanics worked long hours but were paid well. Spracklin would probably have spent the rest of his working life assembling and repairing automobile engines were it not for the tragic death of his older brother William in 1907.

###

---

5 October 2012 interview with Kathy Rappaport

'Willie' Spracklin had been a cause celebre in the boxing world for years, beating opponents on both sides of the border. Known professionally as the 'Windsor Featherweight', he was smaller than his brothers but quick on his feet and packed a vicious punch.

Willie had briefly retired from fighting in November 1906, after his close friend and fellow boxer Mike Ward was killed during a bout in Grand Rapids, Michigan.[6] Friends and boxing fans begged him to reconsider and he acquiesced, but his return to the ring was fated to last less than a year.

On the morning of November 9, 1907, Willie and four friends went duck hunting on Fighting Island, the largest Canadian island on the Detroit River, so named because it had once been a popular spot for holding illegal prizefights. While combing the coastline for waterfowl, a man named Mason saw Willie moving through the reeds, mistook him for a duck, and fired. The bullet entered the young boxer's head and sent him crashing into the swampy water. He

---

[6] *Pittsburgh Press*, November 23, 1906

died days later in the Windsor Hospital without regaining consciousness.7

Willie's death was a heavy blow, but when Leslie Spracklin learned that the duck hunters had been drinking during the Fighting Island expedition, fury underscored his grief. Up until this point, he'd merely avoided liquor and the places that served it. Now, convinced that Willie would still be alive if Mason's judgment hadn't been compromised, Spracklin turned a personal conviction into a public campaign, not caring who he offended in the process.

He started lecturing his co-workers about the evils of drink. If Spracklin suspected a fellow mechanic of imbibing secretly at lunch or coming to work with a hangover, he threatened to report them to management if they didn't mend their ways. His zeal got him into a few post-workday fights but he was big and fast enough to make physical confrontations rare.

The crusade continued unchecked until 1909, when Spracklin finally left Ford.8 He

---

7*Pittsburgh Press,* November 18, 1907

8Interview with Kathy Rappaport

needed a bigger platform that would reach more people, and found it in the Methodist ministry.

CHAPTER 2

Church leaders, women's groups, and pro-temperance politicians had been campaigning against the Canadian liquor trade for decades. The Methodist church, along with the Woman's Christian Temperance Union (WCTU), the Lodges of the Independent Order of Good Templars, the Dominion Alliance, and the Divisions of the Sons of Temperance, spearheaded the movement to make Ontario dry. They refused to endorse the sale of alcohol even under stringent conditions, such as strict licensing requirements. Samuel Chown, general superintendent of the Methodist Church of Canada, proclaimed, "We will have nothing to do with license... We are out to annihilate the trade."

The anti-liquor forces had concern for public welfare on their side, making their stance difficult to dismiss completely. They warned in editorials that alcohol consumption turned "homes into hovels" and caused "feeblemindedness, idiocy, epilepsy and tendencies to all kinds of moral weakness."9 In 1876 the Dominion Alliance released the following declaration of principles:

1. That it is neither right nor politic for the Government to afford legal protection and sanction to any traffic or system that tends to increase crime, to waste the resources of the Dominion, to corrupt the social habits, and to destroy the healths and lives of the people.

2. That the traffic in intoxicating liquors as common beverages is inimical to the true interests of individuals, and destructive of the order and welfare of society, and ought therefore to be prohibited.

3. That the history and results of all legislation in regard to the liquor traffic

---

9 C.H. Gervais, *The Rumrunners: a Prohibition Scrapbook.* (Scarborough: Firefly Books, 1980) p. 10

abundantly prove, that it is impossible satisfactorily to limit or regulate a system so essentially mischievous in its tendencies.

4. That no consideration of private gain or public revenue can justify the upholding of a traffic so thoroughly wrong in principle, so suicidal in policy, and disastrous in its results, as the traffic in intoxicating liquors.

5. That the Legislative Prohibition of the liquor traffic is perfectly compatible with national liberty, and with the claims of justice and legitimate commerce.

6. That the Legislative Prohibition of the liquor traffic would be highly conducive to the development of progressive civilization.

7. That rising above sectarian and party considerations, all good citizens should combine to procure an enactment prohibiting the manufacture and sale of intoxicating beverages, as affording the

most efficient aid in removing the appalling evils of intemperance.10

The spirit that had inspired those words in 1876 was still strong in 1909, when Leslie Spracklin applied to the Methodist ministry and was received on probation. He spent a year travelling the circuit, becoming accustomed to the demands of a pastor's life. After matriculating briefly at Windsor Collegiate, he enrolled at Victoria College's School of Theology in Toronto in 1912. (Two years later his brother Arthur joined him, although military service would call Arthur away in 1918, before he could graduate.)

Victoria College was originally founded in 1832 as the Upper Canada Academy by the Wesleyan Methodist Church. Located in Cobourg, Ontario, it was a liberal arts school that also functioned unofficially as a Methodist seminary. Even after it was renamed Victoria University and relocated to Toronto in 1892, it retained stringent rules that other universities

---

[10] The Journal of the Synod of the Church of England in the Diocese of Huron, Nineteenth Session, June 20-22, 1876. p. 165, 166

had long since dropped, such as a prohibition on dancing.

Victoria College circa 1916. (E.J. Pratt Library)

While at Victoria College, Leslie Spracklin quickly distinguished himself as a sportsman and leader. He held the 'left scrim' position on the college rugby team and joined the Athletic Union Executive. Surrounded by like-minded friends, his often-rigid personality relaxed and a mischievous streak surfaced. When a burglar broke into his room one night, he and his roommate overpowered the man and, while waiting for the police to arrive, amused themselves by putting their prisoner through harmless but humiliating tribulations.11

Having been diminished so often by Babe Trumble, Spracklin was quick to defend victims of bullying. One day he went into the mens' room in one of the campus buildings and found a small group of students surrounding a terrified young man.

"What are you doing to him?" he demanded.

One of the tormentors smirked and brandished a pair of scissors. "We're giving this fairy a haircut."

Their victim had longer hair, which may or may not have been a reflection of his sexuality. But all Spracklin saw was a crowd was menacing a lone individual.

"Why don't you fellows give me a haircut while you're at it, then?" he demanded, balling his large hands into fists.

A melee erupted, with the rowdies getting the worst of it before outside interference arrived. Spracklin apparently remained in touch

---

11 Interview with Kathy Rappaport

with the grateful youth even after they had both graduated.12

Although aggravating, such incidents were rare, and Spracklin enjoyed his time at Victoria College. His entry in the 1916 yearbook reads as follows:

> *Born in Woodstock '86, but raised in Windsor. Machinist '05-'09. Realizing his call, went on circuit '09-'10 and '13-'14. Matric at Windsor Collegiate '12. Victoria '12. "Bob" committee and executive '16. Interested in sports and a jolly friend.*

In March of the same year, Billy Sunday came to Toronto to give a pro-temperance speech. Sunday, a former baseball outfielder turned influential evangelist, was one of the American Prohibition movement's most effective weapons. After warming up his audiences with powerfully delivered gospel music, he would race onstage and deliver an always-memorable performance. During his sermons,

---

12 Interview with Kathy Rappaport

which were colorful ard packed with the slang of the day, Sunday would gyrate, leap onto the pulpit, run back and forth across the stage, and even smash chairs to pieces. Many religious leaders decried him as a loudmouthed show-off, but the crowds kept coming, which was all Sunday cared about.

Leslie and Arthur Spracklin probably attended his appearance on March 8th. Although neither of them would indulge in onstage antics to advocate the temperance cause, both young men understood from Sunday's example that uphill battles were won only when the fighters were prepared to go to extremes. Halfway measures were tantamount to doing nothing at all.

Four years later, Leslie Spracklin would tell a packed courtroom, "The trouble with us (in enforcing the dry laws) is that we haven't been in earnest. The trouble is that we go on a kind of hit and miss plan. There are a lot of people who have something wrong with their spark when it comes to doing something for God. They're hitting on three cylinders. Some people say to me, 'Spracklin, you're hitting your head against a stone wall.' Well, I'd rather bump my head against a stone wall until I bumped my brains out than have it said that I didn't have courage to bump it at all."13

13 *Toronto Daily Star*, Nov. 15, 1920

CHAPTER 3

Sandwich Methodist Church (courtesy of Kathy Rappaport

Upon graduation and ordination in 1916, Spracklin was sent to Romney Township, in

Kent County. He went home to Windsor regularly, his visits becoming more frequent after he met and fell in love with twenty-year-old Myrle Welsh. On June 19, 1917, they married. The couple didn't remain in rural Romney for long: in 1918 Spracklin was transferred to the Methodist church in Sandwich, approximately two miles from downtown Windsor. He and Myrle moved into the parsonage at 698 Sandwich Street and prepared to minister to a community that had known them nearly all their lives.

Spracklin distinguished himself in the pulpit as a spirited opponent of Demon Rum. His anti-liquor sermons were vindictive and sometimes theatrical in their intensity, mixing Bible verses with pointed accusations. But they were also persuasive, because he reported things that he had personally witnessed.

Spracklin often patrolled the streets of Windsor and Sandwich, lurking outside road-houses in his parked car and watching the drunks spill out into the street at all hours. If he spotted local dignitaries in their midst, he did not hesitate to name them from the pulpit the following Sunday.

His zeal created bitter enemies, which did not appear to trouble him. In 1920, after he had become a North American household name, Spracklin said, "If there are any critics, I want to say I stood in the vanguard because I tried to do the work that ought to have been done by the officers of the law in (the) border cities."

That was only partly true. He acted from a sense of duty, but Spracklin's competitive spirit also recognized an opportunity to engage two enemies in battle. The first was the liquor traffic. The second was Beverly Trumble, who now owned the Chappell House, one of the most popular roadhouses in town.

Saloons and roadhouses that served liquor were illegal in Ontario in 1918, but no one seemed to care. To Spracklin's chagrin, the police in the border cities ignored the violations and even patronized the "dens of iniquity", as he called them.

The Ontario Temperance Act (OTA) had been in effect since 1916, when the provincial government passed it as a wartime support measure. Under its statutes, bars and saloons were closed, and no one could "have, keep, give, or consume liquor except in a private dwelling house." The production and sale of strong alcohol was permitted for only medicinal, mechanical, scientific and sacramental purposes. Any establishment wishing to sell the legally approved 2.5 percent beer had to apply for a special license and provide meals, public lavatories for both sexes, and overnight accommodations.

Liquor raid in Elk Lake, Ontario. (Author's Collection)

Ontario residents were used to a certain level of restriction on their leisure activities during the 1910s. On Sundays it was illegal to "buy ice cream, newspapers or a cigar; to play baseball, tennis, or golf; to fish or take a steamboat excursion."14 But banning liquor consumption after the war ended aggravated many people. One member of the Citizen's Liberty League complained, "The Women's Christian Temperance Union are already framing up a number of prohibition laws whereby Canadians will wear bibs and tuckers, curtsy to the Methodist

---

[14] Cheryl Lynn Krasnick Warsh, ed. *Drink in Canada* (Montreal: McGill-Queen's Press, 1993) p. 15

Preacher and be supervised the same as our Anglo-Saxon brothers supervise the inferior races of niggers, Indians, and Coolies. Canadians will officially be placed on a similar footing– a nice standing for a race who proved their fighting value on the fields of France."15

Like most unpopular laws, the Ontario Temperance Act was weakened by public defiance and the difficulty of hiring enforcement agents who could be trusted to do the job without yielding to bribes or threats. The Sandwich-Windsor area posed a special challenge. Its connection to Detroit made it the site of the busiest commercial border crossing in North America, and liquor was a popular commodity.

The OTA had loopholes that the Canadian brewers, distillers, and bootleggers cheerfully took advantage of. Full-strength product could legally be produced for export, so after noting on the customs form that their cargo was destined for the United States, St. Pierre et Miquelon, or Cuba, Ontario captains would leave Canadian shores only to 'short circuit', or

---

15 Jean R. Burnet, *Ethnic Groups in Upper Canada* (Ontario Historical Society Research Publication No. 1, 1972, p. 5

secretly return and unload everything at a remote location near Windsor.

After Prohibition became law in the U.S. in 1920, liquor-laden boats crossed the Detroit River day and night. There were several small islands that could act as hiding spots at the first sign of a government boat, and private docks on both shorelines were attached to underground tunnels for smuggling the cargo inland. In the wintertime, automobiles loaded with booze crawled carefully across the ice, doors open in case the surface cracked and the driver and passengers had to jump out suddenly.

It was dangerous work: cars sometimes fell through the ice, and rival bootleggers and zealous dry agents could be violent when intercepting shipments. But the financial rewards reaped from successful deliveries were a powerful incentive to keep going. An estimated twenty-five percent of the Ontario population near the Detroit River was in the booze smuggling business. During the first seven months of 1920 alone, the Windsor courts collected a quarter of a million dollars in fines from boaters caught with liquor aboard.16

Methodist pastor John Coburn told the Toronto Daily Star, "The traffic in booze at the border is tremendous. Men who were poor a few weeks or months ago are now riding around in cars. Some men are said to make $5000 or $6000 in one shipment. They can afford to pay a $2000 fine."17

Defendants in OTA cases were cheerfully defiant. When W. A. Curran appeared before a judge in May 1920, he claimed that he and his family had consumed 142 bottles of liquor in twelve days. The license inspector who arrested him said that Curran had received 192 bottles in two separate shipments, but a raid turned up only fifty. To avoid the more severe charge of selling contraband, the defendant insisted that everything he had purchased was for home use. He, his parents, his brother, and his sister-in-law drank everything themselves.

---

16 C.H. Gervais, *The Rumrunners: a Prohibition Scrapbook.* (Scarborough: Firefly Books, 1980) p.10

17 *Toronto Daily Star,* July 16, 1920

"But how do you account for the fact that liquor disappeared at the rate of more than 10 bottles a day?" the judge asked.

Curran grinned. "We just licked it up!"

Attorney-General William Raney despaired of bringing the area under control - until the name of Reverend Leslie Spracklin reached him in the summer of 1920.

CHAPTER 4

On the night of June 20, 1920, Spracklin interrupted a meeting of Sandwich's town council and demanded an investigation into the police department. He told the disconcerted councilmen that one night he had gone to Beverly Trumble's Chappell House and counted over thirty drunks coming out while Chief of Police Alois Masters sat on the front steps, "twirling his thumbs."

"This historic town has become a dumping ground for the lowest element; an element which we might as well be rid of and which comes to us from all parts of the United States to obtain what they are looking for: strong drink," Spracklin complained. "They come to the border cities for it and secure it largely in the town of Sandwich. There is a flagrant disregard for the law and so far the police have made no effective efforts to deal with the situation. The streets have become unsafe for our mothers, wives, and daughters on account of the open debauch which is going on here."18

He focused on the Chappell House. Drunken men and, more alarmingly, women came out at all hours, according to Spracklin. He saw one girl "so drunk that she rolled all over the porch" and a man "so loaded with liquor that he had to be helped to the end of the verandah." Girls, he added, "came out in such an intoxicated state that they had to be helped to the automobiles by their escorts, or they would have fallen down the steps."19

The council advised him to put his charges in writing, which was a polite way of brushing him off. When Spracklin tried to appear before the council again on July 5 to protest the lack of corrective action, Mayor E.H. Donnelly ordered him to leave or risk arrest. He reluctantly obeyed, but not before presenting a two-page

---

18 C.H. Gervais, *The Rumrunners: a Prohibition Scrapbook.* (Scarborough: Firefly Books, 1980) p.121

19 Ibid

report that charged the Sandwich police department and the police committee with neglect of duty.

"Under a proper investigation," he wrote, "evidence will be produced to show a widespread disregard of law and a method of enforcement which virtually amounts to a protection of those engaged in law violation."

Receiving no official response to his report, the tenacious pastor faced the council a third time on July 19. After he unleashed another stream of accusations against the roadhouses and the police, a hostile crowd sitting on the rear benches started catcalling and yelling, trying to drown out his words. Spracklin ignored them and kept talking. Mayor Donnelly refused to grant him permission to officially speak and turned a deaf ear when two council members, Haggart and Wright, submitted a motion to let Spracklin address the council. When they protested, Donnelly ruled them out of order.

The council voted to have the police committee investigate all allegations against the department and Chief Masters, which baffled Spracklin and the two councilmen who supported him. Haggart pointed out that the police committee was basically being directed to judge itself, which was ludicrous. He submitted an amendment to have the investigation conducted by an independent tribunal, but it was voted down.

A pro-liquor mob surrounded Spracklin when he left the room. The Toronto Daily Star reported, "The clergyman, with his back to the wall, faced his enemies calmly and told them to come on, as he could use his fists if necessary and that he did not fear them, even if they were fifty to one." Spracklin then passed through the hostile crowd unaided, declaring that he was not afraid to walk home by himself.

Councillor Haggart wasn't surprised at the crowd's reaction. "What do you expect?" he told a reporter. "Ninety percent of them are bootleggers."

Attorney-General William Raney read the press coverage of Spracklin's activities and was impressed by the outspoken minister's dedication to the temperance cause and his fearlessness in exposing violations. By July 1920 so many license inspectors had been fired for dishonesty or cowardice that OTA enforcement was problematic, but Raney believed that hiring the right men would solve the problem.

A.G. Sykes, an honest dry agent with an impressive record, agreed. "It is not the number of men that will clear up the situation, but the honesty and energy of a few tested individuals."

Testing was a mild term for what license inspectors, border patrol officers, and others charged with enforcing the dry laws experienced. Bootleggers offered them immense bribes to overlook alcohol shipments or provide advance warning of raids. Those who did not succumb to temptation were threatened, demoted by corrupt superiors, and even beaten up. In one extreme case, a conscientious American border patrol officer, Daniel Shimel, was offered $50,000 to retire early. When he refused, colleagues who were taking bribes tried to have him killed.

OTA officials complained to Raney that retaining trustworthy officers was an uphill battle: few were willing to risk life and limb for a law that the general public did not appear to want.

Judging from his reaction to the hostile Sandwich mob, the attorney general believed that Leslie Spracklin could be one of the rare exceptions.

Raney wasn't the only one who saw Spracklin's potential. Reporters speculated that it was only a matter of time before the minister's activities received government backing. When they did, the rumrunners would be in for a serious fight. Someone could even get killed, generating headlines that doubled a newspaper's circulation in days.

The reporters couldn't wait.

Weeks passed. Then, on July 27, the Toronto Daily Star trumpeted: SPRACKLIN TO BE ARMED WITH BIG STICK OF LAW.

"Keen, practical, square, energetic, an athlete every inch of him, blazingly indignant at the drunken scenes of lawlessness he has been forced to witness... such a man must have his turn," the paper applauded.

The war was on.

CHAPTER 5

When approached by Raney's office, Spracklin jumped at the chance to become a license inspector. He was still fuming over the town council fiasco, and a government badge would give his campaign a much-needed stamp of authority. But he had one important condition: that he work independently of the existing OTA brass. He suspected most of them of being ineffective at best, corrupt at worst, and did not want to be reined in by superiors with a potentially questionable agenda. Raney readily agreed, and the formal appointment date was set for July 30. Spracklin spent the entire train trip back to Windsor in a state of keen anticipation, like a greyhound awaiting the signal to chase the rabbit.

"I intend to fight to the end," he promised in his first official interview. "I vow and declare that conditions will never be as bad as they have recently been, no matter what kind of personal campaign there is against me."

There would be plenty of them, as it turned out.

On July 29 the Sandwich police committee, predictably, cleared itself of all wrongdoing in connection with Spracklin's allegations. The proceedings were closed to the public, but Beverly Trumble, one of the key witnesses, chatted with reporters during breaks in his testimony. At first he was in a sour mood: when one Toronto journalist asked what type of beer he'd be served at the Chappell House, Trumble's handsome face darkened and he growled, "Poison." Then his sense of proper public relations kicked in, and he relaxed.

It was true that drunken people occasionally came to the Chappell House and created a disturbance, he said, but he dealt with them immediately and could hardly be blamed for what anyone did before their arrival. "The Negros help too," he complained, referring to his black staff. "They smuggle in liquor. I have to search their baggage every day. I was never arrested for selling liquor in my place. The first time (there was trouble) it was because of a waiter. The second time it was because of a porter." Trumble said that he had fired over twenty black waiters since he had been in business.

He acknowledged that the Chappell House used to have an unsavory reputation, but that he'd cleaned it up, and the Sandwich police were not helping him whitewash a rowdy operation.

"Everyone who says that I am in with the police is a liar, and I will say it right to his heart. They don't do me any favors, I can tell you. I treat them like gentlemen any time I see them. That's as far as it goes with me." Concluding the interview, he said, "Anyhow, I'm not going to worry. When we clean up the ministers, there'll be a decent country."[20]

Spracklin did not appear at the hearings. Interviewed afterward, he said, "I gave them my

---

[20] *Toronto Daily Star*, July 30, 1920

answer the night of the council meeting, when they treated me so roughly. At that meeting I absolutely refused to have anything to do with the whole farce. A man would be a fool to expect to get justice from anybody passing judgment on themselves."

He had just returned from an automobile ride throughout the county. A reporter noticed the .32 Colt tucked in his belt and asked about it.

"Father gave it to me today to replace the .22 automatic (I used to have)," Spracklin explained. "I feel that the Good Lord, who has carried me to the ministry and has evidently been instrumental in bringing me here for the cleanup, will see me through without any trouble. But I am going to let them (the bootleggers) know that I mean business." He patted the weapon.

"They will be popping at you from behind a bridge," the reporter warned. But Spracklin reiterated that he was undeterred by the prospect of injury or death.

Told that Babe Trumble had invited him to tour the Chappell House and see for himself that no liquor was being served, he scoffed.

"Why should I go into the Chappell House when asked? The place would be holystoned to perfection."

He had every intention of calling on Trumble, though. Just not when he was expected.

CHAPTER 6

The 'Fighting Parson', as the press now called him, went straight to work on July 30, the very night his appointment took effect. He'd given several interviews throughout the week, warning that Armageddon was en route for the liquor interests, and the bootleggers and roadhouse owners were nervous. A taxi driver commented to newsmen, "There isn't anything doing at all. He's got them all in their rat holes. The word has gone out that Spracklin will be out tonight and there is absolutely not a drop of it (liquor) out."[21]

Spracklin headed straight for two small roadhouses he had been watching for awhile. He and his fellow inspectors found enough full bottles, emptied glasses, and rambunctious

---

[21] *Toronto Daily Star,* July 31, 1920

drunks to lay charges. The proprietors and their customers were belligerent, shouting insults that questioned Spracklin's parentage and intelligence, but the inspectors didn't encounter any actual violence until they descended on a small hotel in Jackson's Corners.

The moment they walked through the public entrance, Spracklin and his two colleagues were intercepted by the proprietor, Louis Menard, Menard's grown son Emile, and two carpenters who'd been working on the premises. When one of the inspectors, a man named Cooran, asked to search the bathroom for contraband, Menard refused, saying that his wife was soaking in the tub.

"Have her answer you from inside then," Spracklin ordered.

When Menard continued to argue, the license inspectors forced the door down. They didn't find Mrs. Menard in a state of undress, but they did see a half-full bottle of whiskey perched on the counter. When Cooran handed it to Spracklin, the two carpenters jumped on the minister, one of them wielding a hammer.

With a speed and violence he had not employed since his days as a boxer and rugby player, Spracklin knocked the hammer out of his assailant's hand and beat the man bloody. Cooran and the other inspector rushed to his assistance, but it was hardly needed. Once the situation was under control, the inspectors delivered their prisoners to the closest police station.

The Crown Attorney fixed a heavy bail amount. "I will not have my officers interfered with," he warned.

The following day, the Windsor Star declared: MR. SPRACKLIN'S FIRST DAY TERRIFIES THE BOOTLEGGERS. 'Terrifies' may have been too strong a word, but he certainly worried them. They knew that he could not be bought off, and scaring him away would be even harder. But if the Fighting Parson proved to be a serious inconvenience to their livelihoods, there were more permanent means of stopping him.

###

The momentum continued. On August 7, Spracklin and Inspectors Cross and Cooran drove to Ford City, where a female bootlegger named 'Mrs. Mechanic' operated. Believing the three men to be customers, she hinted that she had more whiskey in stock than she knew what to do with.

"Care to get rid of it?" Cooran asked, straight-faced.

Delighted, Mrs. Mechanic quoted a price of fifty dollars a case. As Spracklin handed the money over, he added, "But we shall want far more than that. Can you get it?"

"Nothing easier in the world," she beamed, waving her hands. She could get them all the whiskey they wanted, provided she received a commission of three dollars a case.[22]

"Done," the minister declared before placing her under arrest. The woman and her husband were major players in the Ford City liquor trade, and shutting them down was a victory for the dry cause.

---

[22] *Windsor Star*, August 8, 1920

As Spracklin's notoriety spread, he drew reactions that were extreme and sometimes hilarious. When he tried to arrest a well-known Jewish bootlegger after posing as a customer, the man fled the premises, leaped over the back fence and ran, as the Toronto Daily Star put it, "like a mad, wild thing, with the officers in hot pursuit. In his pocket, unfortunately, was a $100 marked government bill, which gave him mercury's classical speed." Knowing that there would be no bargaining with the Fighting Parson, the bootlegger fled to Flint, Michigan, and stayed there.

The bootleg king of Amherstburg, Ontario wasn't as intimidated by the now-famous dry agent. "Tell him that he doesn't come into Amherstburg with his outfit," the gangster growled to a reporter. When the comment was published, Spracklin retorted, "Tell him we're coming." They did, too, much to the cocky gangster's chagrin.

Spracklin's effectiveness made him enemies among the city and provincial police. Some resented being diminished by a civilian, others fretted over lost bribe money. One night, he stopped a Packard with Michigan license plates near the border, suspicious that it might be transporting liquor. The driver and passengers flashed badges that identified them as provincial police officers. One ranted at Spracklin, "You goddamned Methodist preacher, I will not stand for this." The man later apologized, saying that he had been drunk at the time!

Not all raids were successful. Sometimes Spracklin would arrive at a roadhouse or hotel and find the place empty or so sanitized that it made a family restaurant appear decadent. He suspected that the bootleggers had a far-reaching spy system that alerted them whenever raids were scheduled. To prevent such advance warning, he stopped letting anyone know his plan of attack until the last minute. A license inspector might be in the middle of lunch at a Chinese restaurant when the minister would pull up outside. After a team was assembled and the car was en route to its destination, Spracklin would say, "I have something really good, a big thing, boys. What do you say?"

Then he would reveal all. But not a moment before.

Ambivalent judges were also a problem. In September Spracklin arrested fifty-eight year old Oliver Grandmaison for transporting a carload of whiskey. After being convicted of bootlegging, Grandmaison was fined $2,000 and sentenced to a month in jail. His lawyer requested that the jail term be remitted due to his age and the fact that he had a family. The magistrate finally agreed, commenting, "Prohibition has been tried and is a failure. I do not believe that the liquor traffic can be done away with by law. They have been trying to do away with it for several years, but cannot. It's one of the evils we have to contend with."

Undeterred, Raney threw his full support behind his star. He appointed more inspectors for the Essex Region. From this talent pool, Spracklin hand-selected a special squad of 'untouchables', men who were fearless and, it was hoped, incorruptible. One of them was his brother Arthur, a war veteran who had taken a leave of absence from the ministry in order to lend his investigative skills and muscle to the cause. Other members of his core team were brothers William and Stanley Hallam, former soldiers originally from Toronto, and Frank and Gordon Bell.[23]He had no way of knowing it at the time, but two of his men would cause him future embarrassment and tarnish the glow of his accomplishments.

###

The 'Spracklin gang', as the press called the new unit, was relentless. No one was too influential to evade them: in mid-August Spracklin and Stanley Hallam arrested Dr. W. Fred Park, mayor of Amherstburg, and Sam Renaud, a town constable, after 230 cases of whiskey were found in Park's barn. Park tried telling the magistrate that he didn't own the liquor but was merely storing it "in the public interest, so that it might not be stolen", but the skeptical official fined him $1000.[24]

---

[23] C.H. Gervais, *The Rumrunners: a Prohibition Scrapbook.* (Scarborough: Firefly Books, 1980) p. 122

[24] *Border Cities Star,* August 27, 1920

Years later, the rumor arose that Spracklin was so fanatical about catching bootleggers that he even had the cars of his parishioners discreetly searched while he preached to them on Sundays. Given the fact that Methodists weren't likely to be drinking, let alone smuggling, liquor, this persistent story can be dismissed as a fabrication by those eager to have him remembered as a mono-minded zealot.

For river policing, Spracklin asked the provincial government for, and got, a lightning fast motorboat, the Panther II. It came in handy early on the morning of August 26, when they stopped nine men, all Americans, and four booze-laden boats on the Detroit River. Three of the vessels were easily secured but the fourth, a large cruiser called the Eugenia, headed for the U.S. side with the agents in hot pursuit. Spracklin and his men fired on the slower boat, frightening the occupants into halting.

Jubilant, the Fighting Parson told a reporter, "What I have done so far is nothing, absolutely nothing, when compared to what I intend doing. The bigger the men involved, the harder I will press them."

The man he really wanted to press hard was Beverly Trumble, who continued to deride him publicly. In mid-August, Spracklin got his chance.

CHAPTER 7

"I was sitting in my study when I saw the Chappell House truck going down Peter Street with a load of beer," Spracklin would tell a jury six months later. "I ran out and jumped in the government Paige."

He followed it to the Chappell House, which was an impressive two-story building with gabled roofs that gave it a bungalow appearance. A round-shingled cupola perched on the southwest corner and wide verandahs ran along the front and west sides. In the back was a smaller house where the black waiters lived.

Spracklin waited in his car until men came out and started to unload the barrels. Then he approached, badge in hand. He asked a black employee whose beer it was, but the frightened man stammered that he didn't know.

A few minutes later, Trumble pulled up in his roadster. Spracklin nodded at the beer-laden truck.

"Do you know anything about this, Bev?"

The roadhouse owner, irritated at finding his old rival there in an official capacity, said, "No."

When Spracklin asked to search his car, Trumble stiffened. "I'll be damned if I let you search my car without a warrant."

"Bev, I don't require a warrant to search your car."

"Well, you'll (need to) have one to search mine."

Before the situation could escalate, Trumble's attractive brunette wife, Lulu, came out to see what the problem was. Over her husband's protests, she opened the trunk of the roadster and let the minister see that no liquor was inside. Spracklin could only confiscate the beer, which technically could have belonged to anyone with access to the truck.

Trumble was still furious. "You are nothing but a low-down cur," he hissed. As the minister drove away, the roadhouse owner stood in his yard and shouted, "You'll get yours. I know damned well!"25

It wasn't the easy takedown that Spracklin had been hoping for, but he'd embarrassed Babe Trumble in front of the latter's wife and employees. That would have to do until the next time.

###

Trumble wasn't the only liquor dealer who was angry with the Fighting Parson by August 1920. Threats arrived at the parsonage via phone and mail almost daily, some of them directed at his family. "All through the summer months, it was impossible to sit on the porch with my wife," Spracklin later recalled. "Every night... we had to draw the shades and sit behind closed doors so that no shadows would be thrown on the blinds." Whenever strangers arrived at the door, he would arm himself before undoing the lock.

---

25 *Toronto Daily Star*, February 24, 1921

During raids Spracklin was frequently attacked but, as the Windsor Star put it, the minister's physique, "hardened by years of toil in a machine shop, lent itself admirably to the rough and tumble; in fact, too readily for his opponents." Using techniques he'd learned as a boxing student, he would strike fast and hard, his blows so well placed that some prisoners required medical treatment afterward.

He had a few close calls: in early September he was overpowered and thrown into a canal outside the community of LaSalle. Spracklin managed to swim to safety, cold and bruised but defiant. He may have been remembering this incident when he roared down the Detroit River in his government speedboat the following month, slicing a bootlegger vessel in two and leaving the occupants to swim to shore.

The Fighting Parson's crusade, which was followed by the border cities press like an exciting soap opera, had a galvanizing effect on the American side of the Detroit River. Not wanting to look passive in comparison, custom officers and dry agents started coordinating efforts with the police departments of the riverside towns, such as Wyandotte, Ecorse, and Trenton. Assistant U.S. District Attorney Polozker had long suspected connivance between the bootleggers and police officers in these communities, and was determined to stop it.

According to Polozker, a policeman in Ecorse commented to his chief, "I think it is about time we raided someone down here. You hear what they are saying about us."

The chief responded, "Better raid them all, I guess. Don't you think?"

The officer gaped. "Raid them all? Well, if you are going to raid them all, here's my badge."

Incredibly, Windsor mayor Blake Winter argued that his city was being shown in a bad light. When reporters asked him if he was going to mimic Detroit's recent venture and buy speedboats to intercept rumrunners on the river, he complained, "Windsor is getting the reputation of being the point where all this whiskey is coming and being distributed from, but it is not Windsor at all." He added that the city "would not be the Jonah for the federal government."26

While Winter was denying that boats were necessary to combat rumrunners, Spracklin was proving him wrong. On September 1, the minister and one of his squad members, Stanley Hallam, spied a man loading cases of whiskey onto a launch. They stopped their car, jumped out, and ordered him to surrender. The rumrunner leaped into his boat and hightailed it to Detroit, the inspectors' bullets harmlessly cutting the water around him. He left behind a new car and five cases of whiskey, but for Spracklin, they were a small consolation prize. He wanted prisoners, not just property.

As the Fighting Parson's victory total rose, the deluge of threats turned into real attempts on his life. The 'Canadian Briefs' section of the August 25, 1920 edition of the Toronto Daily Star noted, "Rev. Mr. Spracklin, of Windsor, who is acting as a license inspector, was shot at while arresting four men and confiscating their liquor." Weeks later, on October 4, drive-by

---

26 *Toronto Daily Star,* August 9, 1920

shooters emptied their weapons into his parsonage, nearly hitting a former police officer who had been visiting. On Halloween they struck again, barely missing Myrle Spracklin and forcing the squad members and their wives to take shelter in a Walkerville hotel. In early November, saboteurs connected wires to the gasoline supply in his speedboat, but their handiwork was discovered in time to avert disaster.27

He also had enemies among the OTA upper echelon: men who resented his success or the fact that he didn't answer to any of them, or both. As summer cooled into fall, one of them decided to use the government to get rid of him.

---

27 *Utica Morning Telegram*, November 9, 1920

CHAPTER 8

M.N. Mousseau was an Essex Region license inspector who had been appointed long before Spracklin. Resenting the free rein that the pastor enjoyed, he went before the Board of License Commissioners on October 21 and threatened to quit unless the Fighting Parson's appointment was revoked. One of his complaints was that Stanley and William Hallam, members of the minister's squad, were nothing but thugs empowered by the government.

There may have been some merit to that accusation. A retired Windsor police officer told author C.H. Gervais in 1980 that the Hallam brothers were "punks". They may not have accepted bribes, but they manhandled prisoners during raids, committed unnecessary property damage, and were just as fond of liquor as the people they arrested. It was also alleged that both brothers pocketed valuables found in cupboards and drawers that they searched. Spracklin eventually dismissed them, but not before their antics gave Mousseau and Spracklin's other detractors a legitimate cause for complaint. 28

By late October the conflict between Spracklin and Mousseau escalated all the way to the Ontario Temperance Act Committee, which summoned them both to Toronto. Before boarding the midnight train on November 2nd, Mousseau spoke to a reporter from the Border Cities Era.

---

[28] In June 1921 William and Stanley were tried for assault and robbery. A man named Frank King claimed that on September 12, 1920 the Hallams held him up at gunpoint while he and some partners were loading liquor onto a sleigh and stole the delivery. They insisted that they had been in Toronto at the time, but failed to prove their alibi. Stanley Hallam also went to trial in May 1921 on a manslaughter charge in connection with the accidental shooting death of Ruby Cross in Toronto. When the Crown prosecutor asked him if he had a temper, Hallam shrugged and said, "Yes."

[28]"It easily gets the better of you?"

[28]"Yes."

"Tell the Era readers to pray that the good Lord may save Brother Spracklin from his 'friends' and himself. There are troubled times ahead for him." He added that Spracklin was "no good" as an OTA agent and that the present popular contempt for the dry laws could be blamed on the antics of Spracklin and his men.

Mousseau had collected affidavits from disgruntled survivors of Spracklin raids, and when the hearings began, he presented them to the committeemen as evidence that the Fighting Parson was a loose cannon.

Spracklin coolly responded to each charge. Told that a woman whom he had arrested claimed that $100 had been stolen from her in the process, he answered that the amount lost had actually been $57, and that she had dropped her purse while resisting capture. He added that he had allowed her to pick up the money before anyone else could dive for it.

Another affidavit charged his squad with breaking into a hotel. Spracklin said that he and his men had found the place's front doors locked but could see lights in upstairs windows and hear what sounded like a boozy party in full swing, giving them probable cause for a search. One of his men climbed onto the verandah, slipped into the hotel through an unlocked window, and let everyone else in.

The affidavit also stated that the proprietor's wife had been threatened with a gun. Spracklin explained that unbeknownst to him, one of his officers had brought along an empty revolver as a protective bluff, and the woman had been frightened by it when the officer pointed it at the partygoers. Eight empty whiskey bottles had been found, cementing Spracklin's suspicion that the hotel was serving liquor.

One of the committee members asked him if it was true that he carried a skeleton key to get into houses at night for the purpose of searching them. Spracklin denied it. "There are many things for which I have been blamed that I knew nothing about until they came out in the paper," he complained.

He admitted to carrying around blank search warrants because in his opinion, bootlegging could not be combated effectively unless warrants were immediately obtainable.

"Why not have martial law and be done with it?" protested a commissioner.

"Well, you'll have that unless the conditions are soon cleared up," Spracklin answered.

In conclusion, he told the committee, "I don't want this miserable job for the enforcement of the Act, with all the risks I am taking and the disruption of my home, unless I can go back tonight or tomorrow feeling that I have the absolute confidence of this committee and the government."

Then it was Mousseau's turn. He complained about the current decentralization of authority, which made it impossible to enforce the OTA as a collective force. Everyone seemed willing to work together, he admitted, "but everyone feels he is master of his own sphere. I feel that as license inspector I should be in command of all the men, Mr. Spracklin included. While Mr. Spracklin desires to cooperate with me, he still reserves the right to go the way he likes." Anxious to portray himself as beneficent, he said, "Mr. Spracklin has disturbed the bootleggers and roadhouses a great deal, but he could have done better if there had been coordination."

Mousseau also denounced Spracklin for using firearms, declaring that it was better to let a boatload of booze get away than risk killing someone. Even a Member of Parliament warned the minister, "That gun will get you in trouble sometime."

In rebuttal, Spracklin presented the number of convictions that his squad had obtained. His evidence and eloquence impressed the committee, which threw itself behind him one hundred percent.

Committee chairman J.D. Flavelle stated afterward, "No other place is as bad as Essex (for temperance violations), therefore extreme measures must be taken where there are extreme conditions…. I think the ends justify the means."

It was a short-lived victory. Three days later, on November 6, 1920, Spracklin's gun got him into trouble at last.

CHAPTER 9

On the night of November 6, Spracklin went to bed shortly after midnight. He was exhausted after a long workday. During his rounds he had driven past the Chappell House four times and seen cars parked along the street and signs of activity, but nothing that justified a search. Not long after he retired, one of his squad members telephoned to report that their patrol car had broken down outside the city. Spracklin, who was still an adept mechanic, agreed to go and assist.

At around 3:30 a.m. he and his men were passing the Chappell House on their return journey when they spied a man lying motionless and bleeding on the front steps. They pulled over to investigate. Spracklin and county constable Mark Heaton (who was an occasional squad member) approached first, followed by Frank and Gordon Bell.

Spracklin hoped that this would be his chance to get something on Babe Trumble. The roadhouse owner had recently accosted the minister's sister, Evelyn, in a public park and told her, "He (Spracklin) wants to get off the job before he gets killed." Soon afterward, Spracklin and his men were searching a hotel called the Dominion House when Trumble, who had been present, sneered, "I don't care whether you are an officer or a preacher or what you are. Come outside and I'll lick you in a short time." Spracklin pushed him aside, stating tersely that he wasn't interested in a brawl. Afterward, as the squad was driving away, Trumble shouted after them, "I'll get you yet!"

As the officers approached the injured man, Trumble came outside. (By other accounts, he was already outside.) He and Spracklin exchanged wary greetings before the minister asked, "What is the trouble (here), Bev?"

Trumble shrugged. "It's only a little thing."

The man, a local bootlegger named Ernest Deslippe, moaned that he had been beaten over the head and thrown out of the hotel. Spracklin assisted Deslippe over to a streetlight so he could see his injuries more clearly. Smelling liquor on the man's breath, the minister recognized an opportunity to search the Chappell House at last.

"This is too bad, Ernie," he said. "Some of your own bunch may have beaten you up. No matter how hard I fight you as an officer, this is a dirty shame."

Trumble, in the meantime, had gone back inside. After telling Deslippe to stay put, Spracklin and his men tried to enter the hotel, only to find the door now locked. Demands for admittance were greeted with mocking laughter from the men inside. One of them jeered, "You can't get in!"

A furious Spracklin, accompanied by Mark Heaton, found an open window leading into the hotel dining room and climbed into the building. They went into the barroom, where Bill Morton, one of Trumble's associates, was sitting with some other men.

Spracklin glared at them. "Too bad, boys. Some of you have beaten up Ernie Deslippe," he said.

Anxious to get the license officers out of the hotel, Morton made a placating gesture and replied, "I take the blame, Les. Let us take him home."

Spracklin shook his head. "I fight you fellows pretty hard, but it's a fright for you to beat your own men up."

While Heaton stood guard in the doorway, Spracklin went behind the bar to search for liquor. A large man in a blue suit stepped in front of him.

"Are you Mr. Spracklin?" Upon receiving an answer in the affirmative, the man beamed. "Let me shake hands with you. I haven't seen you in sixteen years."

Spracklin shook hands, but suspected that he was being stalled, as he couldn't recall seeing the friendly stranger before. He was on the verge of resuming the search when the swing doors leading into the room swayed on their hinges and an angry voice boomed, "Let me see your badges, every one of you. I'll shoot every one of you if you don't show them to me."

Looking in the direction of the noise, Spracklin saw Trumble standing in the hallway, waving a gun at Frank and Gordon Bell. The doors swung closed, blocking off his view, but he could hear the confrontation progress from the hallway to the hotel kitchen. He drew his automatic and, accompanied by Heaton, went through the roadhouse in search of Trumble, finally locating him in a private dining room.

Spracklin later claimed that Trumble had been waving a gun and foaming with rage when they encountered each other in the dining room. When Heaton tried to disarm the yelling man, one of the roadhouse employees grabbed the officer and dragged him back. Trumble was heard shouting, "Spracklin, I'll shoot you." He never had the chance- the minister, who'd drawn his own weapon, was faster on the trigger.

The bullet cut Trumble's femoral artery in two, causing him to bleed to death in just twenty-five minutes. Dr. W.C. Pepin, who later conducted the post-mortem, said that the bullet had entered Trumble's body at the left side of the groin, passed through the abdominal cavity and lower bowel, and cut the artery before exiting via the right thigh. He speculated that the roadhouse owner might have lived were it not for the arterial wound.

While Trumble's wife and employees clustered around the fallen man, Spracklin hurried out of the Chappell House. He and a squad member named Bennett, whose car he had fixed, waited behind a refreshment store until the doctors and Sandwich police arrived. Then, after stopping at the home of his in-laws and asking them to go to Myrle, he gave himself up to the Windsor police. The shooting had taken place in Sandwich, but given his accusations against Chief Alois Masters and the Sandwich department in July, Spracklin had no desire to fall into their hands.

The morning editions trumpeted the news of Trumble's death. Told that he would be held pending an investigation by the crown attorney, Spracklin calmly acquiesced. He may not have known it at the time, but his career as a license inspector was now dead too.

CHAPTER 10

Spracklin en route to the inquest. (Courtesy of the Windsor Star)

The inquest was held on the evening of November 6th. Spracklin testified that Trumble had pressed a gun to his stomach and shouted, "Damn you, Spracklin, I'm going to shoot you."

"I knew then that it was his life or mine," the pale but defiant minister concluded. Constable Heaton and the other squad members corroborated his version of events.

Lulu Trumble, now a pregnant widow, rebutted their testimony. She said that on the night of the shooting she had been sick in bed. Her husband had been preparing a hot water bottle for her when someone knocked on the door and said that Spracklin was there and wanted to see Trumble.

"He went into the private dining room with the hot water bottle in one hand and a cigarette in the other," she testified. "I got right up and went in behind (Trumble). I saw five or six men blocking both doorways. They all had guns in their hands."

Mrs. Trumble claimed that her husband demanded to see a search warrant. "(He) then walked over to Spracklin. They were about three or four feet apart. That's all I remember. The shot was then fired. That's all that was said. It was all over in five minutes."

"Did your husband have a revolver?" Crown Attorney Rodd asked.

"No, he merely had a cigarette in his hand. He had laid the hot water bottle on the table." She told the court that Trumble's last words to Spracklin were "You dog, you have shot me!"

The inquest was adjourned until Monday so that witnesses who hadn't been located in time for the proceedings could be brought in. Leslie and Myrle Spracklin left immediately for Chatham, where they stayed at the home of Rev. Robert Hicks, who had married them four years previously.

Mrs. Charity Spracklin, the minister's mother, spoke to reporters at her home in Windsor. "It just seemed to have been fate," she said as she showed them a photo that hung in her dining room. The newsmen stared: the picture, which had been taken at the Fort Erie race track years ago, showed Beverly Trumble posing with the long-dead Willie Spracklin.

"I knew Beverly in long clothes," Mrs. Spracklin said sadly. "We used to visit the Trumbles of an evening. There is only one thing of which I am glad: that Beverly's mother is not alive to have this tragedy thrust upon her. I sympathize with the Trumbles because they sympathized with me when my son was killed."

The Detroit News wrote, "Mrs. Spracklin for the last four months has dreaded the ring of the telephone, the knock on the door, for with each she anticipated the news that her boy, Leslie Spracklin, had been killed. Letters threatening to kill Spracklin were sent to (her home) at 145 Cameron Avenue each week. They went into the fire as soon as they were opened, but the threats remained in the mother's mind."29

On the afternoon of November 8, Beverly Trumble was laid to rest in the family mausoleum at Windsor Grove cemetery. His father, ex-alderman Hamilton Trumble, had reacted to the news of his son's death by shouting threats that were reproduced in newspapers all over the country. Once the madness of grief subsided, he and the rest of the family shunned all

---

29 *Detroit News*, November 9, 1920

publicity and focused on giving Beverly Trumble a worthy funeral.

The wake was held at the senior Trumble's home. Hundreds came to pay their respects, and the oak casket was soon buried beneath a mountain of wreaths. After the funeral services concluded, the cortege proceeded slowly to the cemetery. So many floral arrangements had been sent that special cars were required to transport them.

The Chappell House was temporarily closed for business, a state advertised rather poignantly by a card on the front door that read, "Closed on account of the death of Beverly Trumble."

The inquest resumed that evening. A Winnipeg man named Ed Smith, who'd assisted the wounded Trumble until medical help could arrive, had originally told the police that the roadhouse owner had not been armed. But Dr. J.W. Beasley, one of two doctors who arrived soon after the shooting, testified that Smith had given him a different story.

"He said that Mr. Trumble had a gun," the doctor stated. The second physician, Dr. V.C. Mills, said that Smith had told him the same thing.

There was good reason to believe that retaliation would be forthcoming from Babe Trumble's gangster friends. "They say they'll get you, even if they have to hire Italian bandits from Detroit," a reporter whispered to Spracklin during a lull in the proceedings. The minister replied simply, "They may."

When all testimony concluded, Coroner Labelle said to the jury, "It is the saddest inquiry that I have had to deal with in my life, and it is occupying the attention of the whole province and the Dominion from the Atlantic to the Pacific. There is no doubt that a stigma has been laid on Essex County and I... can say that bootlegging is wrong in any community. Whether Mr. Spracklin is right or wrong is for you to say. But I think that he deserves credit for the way that he has been carrying on the work against that evil force."

While waiting for the verdict, Spracklin showed the only sign of nervousness since the proceedings began. The crowds in the courtroom and outside on Sandwich Street were also tense with anticipation.

At 11:15 p.m., the jury delivered its decision.

"We, your coroner's jury, find that Beverly Trumble came to his death from a bullet fired from an automatic pistol by J.O.L. Spracklin, license inspector, in self-defense at around 3:30 a.m. on November 6, 1920, at the Chappell House in the town of Sandwich."

Pale with relief, Spracklin hugged his elderly father, who'd remained at his side constantly, and said, "It's all right, Dad. It would have been all right anyway, even if they had returned a different verdict, as I would have been acquitted in the end."

Crown Attorney Rodd seemed to approve of the jury's decision. During his closing remarks, he'd confirmed the right of an officer to fill out blank search warrants and search a public house at his discretion. He also stated that a man who obstructed officers in their lawful duty committed one of the gravest breaches of the law.

Rodd made special arrangements to get Spracklin and his supporters safely out of the building, but as it turned out, there was little need for precautions. A cold drizzle had caused the crowds outside to disperse, and there was no disorderly conduct on the part of the people who remained. No violence broke out until later that night, when a car stopped outside Spracklin's home and emptied half a dozen bullets into it.

The next day, Spracklin announced that he was organizing his men under the leadership of his brother Arthur, whose record as a license officer was almost as impressive as his own. Then he planned to go away with his wife for a month and recover from the toll that had been taken on his nerves and energy.

"I am pretty well tired out," he admitted to a reporter from the Windsor Star as they sat together at his parents' house. That night, he and

Myrle left for Chatham, where their old friend Reverend Robert Hicks had opened his home to them.

The Fighting Parson's supporters feared for his safety: when one of his friends, who was temporarily conducting services at the Sandwich Methodist Church in his stead, prayed, "Bless the pastor of this church at this time", tears filled the eyes of many congregants.

After a brief meeting, the Methodist ministers of the Windsor area told the press that they were "greatly gratified in the speedy and authoritative justification of the Reverend J.O.L. Spracklin as touching the altogether regrettable tragedy in Sandwich.... We also express our abiding confidence in the Christian manhood, integrity, and zeal of Reverend J.O.L. Spracklin in the exercise of the serious task assigned to him by the government in guarding (the) vital interests of the community at this critical juncture of provincial events."[30]

Both Canadian and American newspapers published editorials congratulating him for the

---

[30] *Montreal Gazette*, November 10, 1920

war he had waged against bootleggers. "Probably no public official in the history of the community has suffered more criticism and risked his health and life more often in the pursuit of duty," the Border Cities Star noted on November 13.

Although exonerated by the coroner's jury, Spracklin wasn't out of the woods yet. As the Toronto Daily Star pointed out the day after the inquest, "The law does not necessarily halt a prosecution because a coroner's verdict acquits a person of manslaughter or murder. A number of cases were cited in which prosecutions were ordered by crown attorneys notwithstanding inquest verdicts favorable to the accused.... It is understood the matter will be left to the discretion of the local authorities."

Crown Attorney Rodd wasn't inclined to prosecute, as evidenced by the dismissal of the Supreme Court Assize grand jury, which had been ordered to remain in session until a decision was made. Spracklin appeared to be disappointed.

"Personally, I should prefer a trial," he told reporters on November 10. "It would settle everything and leave no room for suspicion.... I want the thing settled and all publicity stopped."

Rodd may not have wished to pursue Spracklin, but Lulu Trumble had other ideas.

CHAPTER 11

Arthur Spracklin (E.J. Pratt Library)

Not wanting the bootleggers to get cocky in his brother's absence, Arthur Spracklin told a reporter, "We are not by any means dropping our campaign against rum-running. This would be no time for the whiskey ring to think for a minute that we were yellow."

The warning was reprinted all over the country. A Toronto Daily Star reporter wrote on November 9, "No armistice will be made with the bootleggers by the Spracklin brothers."

Arthur Spracklin showed remarkable initiative once he assumed command of his brother's squad. He and United States Prohibition officials organized a joint effort to battle the liquor traffic on the Detroit River: he detailed one of his men to accompany American officers in their patrol boat, while the Americans supplied an agent to work with the Canadians during river surveillance.

"By this scheme, each party has jurisdiction over both Canadian and American waters, enabling them to follow the smugglers' launches into the slips on both sides of the border," the Toronto Daily Star informed its readers. It was a huge step forward in dry law enforcement: rumrunners had routinely escaped prosecution by fleeing to the opposite shore, where the Prohibition or customs agents who were chasing them had no jurisdiction.

Not all of the headlines that Arthur Spracklin made were positive. On November 16,

Attorney-General Raney received the following telegram from A.F. Healy, lawyer and former president of the Windsor Chamber of Commerce.

> *Arthur Spracklin assaulted W.L. Messenger, manager of the Canadian Postum Cereal Company and C.C. Chauvin, former Reeve of Sandwich West, at 6:30 p.m. on Saturday night. The men were on their way home from an auction sale at the time. Officers refused to show badge or warrant and pulled a gun. Both men are highly respectable citizens and not suspected of being connected with the liquor traffic. Responsibility for further deaths in this district is up to you.*

Raney sent the following reply.

> *Wire received. Have asked statement from Mr. Spracklin. Will advise chairman of board to suggest caution to officers, but on the other hand, citizens ought not to be too sensitive. I say this because the*

dispatch in this morning's Globe puts a color on the affair rather different from your telegram.

Spracklin told Raney that they'd stopped the automobile during a routine roadside inspection. Messenger refused to let them search it for liquor, saying that he was not a bootlegger. When they insisted, he shouted that the inspectors had no right to interfere with him. Spracklin snapped a pair of handcuffs on him and another officer seized Chauvin by the arm to prevent him from running. The situation was finally defused when Messenger and Chauvin calmed down and properly identified themselves, at which point they were released.31

Raney accepted Arthur Spracklin's version of events and did nothing further. But privately he worried, especially about the Fighting Parson. Although public opinion appeared to be in the Spracklin's favor, Raney worried that the Trumble shooting would be held up as an

---

31 *Windsor Star*, November 16, 1920

example of overzealous and dangerous OTA enforcement, threatening the future of the Act itself.

******

Speculation arose over whether Leslie Spracklin would continue as a license inspector for the Essex region, despite the verdict of the coroner's jury. Crown Attorney Rodd said, "He will go right on with his work cleaning up, and it will be pushed stronger than ever before. This is the desire of the government."

The Detroit Free Press hinted that Spracklin would probably be removed from the ministry for taking a life, an allegation that Methodist ministry representatives in both Windsor and Detroit hotly denied. "There is not a word of truth in the report," said Dr. H.W. Craws. "It is one of the wild rumors circulated since the events.... There is no such clause in the Methodist doctrine."

Reverend H. E. Gullen of the West Grand Boulevard Methodist Church in Detroit agreed. "There isn't anything in the world to prevent him from holding his pulpit."

Rumor ran rampant that Spracklin would be resigning, but he dispelled it. "Reports that I will resign have been circulated by persons in whose breasts the wish is father to the thought," he said. "I have never had any intention of resigning and have returned to the border determined to carry on the work in which I have been engaged for some months past."

Therefore people were surprised when the border cities newspapers announced on November 13 that Spracklin had tendered his resignation as leader of the special squad. He cited fatigue and his wife's failing health as the reasons. He and Arthur Spracklin both declared themselves willing to work under his replacement should they be needed. As it turned out, they weren't: at the end of November, Attorney-General Raney disbanded the squad and replaced his former protégé with Superintendent W.J. Lannin, former chief of the Stratford, Ontario police department.

Spracklin took the dismissal with good grace, but wanted it known that he had done his best to cope with an impossible situation. He and Myrle went to Exeter, Ontario, where he spoke to a crowd of over 1600 at the James Street Methodist Church.

"All I have been trying to do has been to do my duty to my God, my church, and the people of this province. If there are any critics, I have only this to say: that I did not seek the position, and I stood in the vanguard because I tried to do the work that ought to have been done by the officers of the law in those border cities."

Addressing those who might be inclined to dismiss the stories of drunkenness and corruption in the border cities, he said, "I want to say that conditions down there have been, and are, so abnormal as to make some of us get into the fight so that our wives, our daughters, and our sisters would even be safe on the streets.... We'll have to answer some day for their wave of cutthroats, pickpockets, and thugs, with which they are deluged at present. We'll have to answer some day for letting rum pour across the river as we have been doing."

He reminded his listeners about the upcoming referendum to prohibit the import of liquor into Ontario. "We are going to hit old John Barleycorn so hard that no government will be able...to dump the cursed stuff back on us when (a majority of) 400,00 in this province has said they don't want it."

While he was preaching to packed churches, Lulu Trumble's lawyers were petitioning the Attorney General to charge Spracklin with manslaughter and put him on trial. When the minister heard about their intentions, he lessened Raney's burden by encouraging him to acquiesce. He insisted that he wanted to prove his innocence once and for all. Spracklin was arraigned on November 20, and released on $10,000 bail. The trial date was set for February 21, 1921.

The Toronto Daily Star, while appreciating the Fighting Parson's desire to clear his name, published an editorial on November 22 that excoriated the Trumble camp and its supporters.

The Case of Mr. Spracklin

People who charge the Drury government with incompetency for not preventing rum-running on the border and in the next breath want the Reverend J.O.L. Spracklin punished for shooting a man in self-defense while performing his duties as license officer are simply running with the hares and hunting with the hounds.

It is un-British for the people, through their Government, to appoint any man to the task of enforcing their laws against a gang of desperate such as have been disgracing the good name of Canada in Essex and Kent, and then to clamour for his prosecution when, being menaced with a revolver, he shoots first.

Not a thirst for notoriety, but decent citizenship led Mr. Spracklin to take over the dangerous and irksome duties of a license officer. Having criticized the lax enforcement of the law he could not well refuse to accept the challenge to try his own hand at it. And it is not heroics, but a simple fact to state that since he got to work effectively repeated efforts have been made on his life, and he has moved about in constant peril. To sneer at such observations is to show utter lack of appreciation of the sacrifices made by a brave man in the service of the community.

Law-breakers in the border communities are so alarmed by the efficiency of Mr. Spracklin as *a license officer that they will stop at nothing to end his career as such. Each time he was called to Toronto they were in high glee because it gave them an opportunity to add to their illegal gains. And if they can put him on trial for his life and have him kept from his duties for a period of months or removed from his position, they would be delighted.*

A man does not need to be in personal sympathy with the OTA to respect Mr. Spracklin as a real man and as one who should have the support of all law-abiding citizens in the present crisis. The talk about there being one law for a parson and another for an ordinary citizen is nonsense.

CHAPTER 12

At the end of December 1920, Spracklin was back in court to respond to charges that he had trespassed on the private yacht of a local lawyer during a search for a suspected booze cache.

Oscar Fleming, who resided in Windsor, claimed that on September 17, 1920, his son was hosting a party aboard the family's yacht. After the boat dropped anchor between Belle Island and Peche Island, the Panther II, which had been following with its lights dimmed to avoid detection, pulled up. Spracklin, accompanied by the Hallam brothers and two other inspectors, climbed aboard. Fleming's son complained, "Mr. Spracklin appeared in the cabin… with a flashlight in his left hand. His right hand was in his coat pocket." The pastor inquired who owned the pleasure boat, and when informed that it belonged to the Flemings, admitted that he would not have stopped it had he known. He searched the yacht anyway, with the Hallams clutching their revolvers and watching closely.32

Chief Justice R.M. Meredith, who presided over the case, condemned Spracklin's behavior, commenting, "He showed unwisdom." The judge conceded that the OTA allowed license officers to search vehicles on public highways for bootleg liquor, but a boat was a different matter: there had to be actual evidence of alcohol smuggling or consumption. He fined the minister $500 in damages. Spracklin appealed the verdict to the Second Appellate Court in April, but it upheld the original decision.

In the meantime, the trial date drew closer. Finally, on the Sunday before it was due to begin, Spracklin addressed his congregation. Reverend Arthur Barker of the Howard Avenue Church had been supplying for him since the shooting, but now he wanted to speak publicly to those who had supported him for so long.

---

[32] Chad Fraser, *Lake Erie Stories: Struggle and Survival on a Freshwater Ocean.* (Toronto: Dundurn Press, 2008) p. 190

"I will say this," he declared in a voice thick with emotion, "I hope to be with you next Sunday."

On February 21, spectators began lining up outside the Sandwich courthouse at 6:30 a.m. Over six hundred had to be turned away. Prospective assassins, determined to avenge Beverly Trumble, may have tried to get access to the courtroom. In his book, The Rumrunners, C.H. Gervais wrote, "A spectator at that trial, in an interview, reported that whole bins of guns were collected by the police from spectators pressing to get a seat."

Hamilton Trumble, father of the slain man, attempted to barge into the sheriff's office where Spracklin was being held. "Let me see the murderer!" he shouted. "I'll get you yet!" Sheriff's officers separated them and escorted Mr. Trumble away.[33]

---

[33] *Windsor Star*, February 21, 1921

Sir William Mulock presided. A. Monroe Grier, K.C., appeared for the Crown. He had been assigned to prosecute the case after Mrs. Trumble's lawyers petitioned the Attorney General to replace Crown Attorney Rodd, who had been openly partial to the defendant. R.L. Brackin was chief counsel for Spracklin.

Lulu Trumble, the prosecution's first witness, repeated that her husband had no gun when Spracklin confronted him. In fact, she insisted, he didn't even own one. Brackin reminded her that only a year before, Trumble had taken a cash register to a repairman to be fixed, and in a fit of rage, put a pistol to the frightened man's head, demanding that he do it "or else." She denied it, saying, "My husband owned rifles, never a handgun."

Lulu Trumble and her two young sons (Courtesy of the Windsor Star)

Then it was time for the defense. A toolmaker named Seaman Held recollected the time Beverly Trumble interfered with Spracklin's search of the Dominion Hotel. "Trumble had been very angry," Held testified. "(He said) I don't care whether you are an officer, a preacher, or what you are, I'll wallop you. Come out on the street and I'll show you." Robert Ballantyne, a tailor, contradicted Lulu Trumble's claim that her husband had never owned a handgun. He said that Trumble had visited his shop two years ago and, while trying on clothes, took a pistol and a handkerchief out of his pocket. John Duggan, an amateur gun-smith, remembered repairing a .38 Smith and Wesson police revolver for Trumble two months before the fatal shooting.

At 7:15 p.m., Leslie Spracklin took the stand. Grier said that he would waive all objections to minor irrelevant details so that the jury could have a thorough understanding of the events leading up to Trumble's death. But when Spracklin recounted the drunken scenes he had witnessed outside the Chappell House and his subsequent appearance before the Sandwich town council, Sir Mulock interrupted him.

"I don't see what that has to do with the trial. It is irrelevant."

Brackin protested that Mrs. Trumble had brought up the town council meeting during her testimony, complaining that it had affected her husband's business. He said that it was a plausible motive for the dead man's hostility toward Spracklin. But Sir Mulock maintained his objection and Spracklin continued. When he finally testified about the shooting, he could barely contain his emotion. He recounted how

Trumble had cursed him and pointed a gun at him, saying, "Spracklin, I'll shoot you."

"While (he was) saying this, I swung my gun from the upraised position to the hip." Mouth trembling and tears in his eyes, Spracklin said, "I pulled the trigger."

Brackin said gently, "Now, at the time that Trumble said, 'I'll shoot you', you looked into his eyes. What was your honest opinion of his intentions?"

"I believed thoroughly that he was going to carry out his threat."

Bootlegger Jack Bannon, who later did time in Kingston Penitentiary for the 1934 kidnapping of Canadian beer tycoon John Labatt, dropped a bombshell on February 23. He told an open-mouthed audience that he saw Lulu Trumble snatch a handgun from her dying husband's grip.

Spracklin's supporters instantly applauded, which angered Sir Mulock. He called the sheriff to the bench and ordered, "Arrest those people who made that demonstration for contempt of court." Facing the audience, he declared, "Those men, if they were men who clapped, stand up."

No one stood.

Grier recalled Lulu Trumble.

"I just want to ask you two or three questions," he said. "It has been stated during the trial that after the shooting, you were seen standing in the same room with a pistol in your hand. What do you say about that?"

"It was not so."

"There is not a word of truth in it?"

"Not a word." The widow glared over at Spracklin. "If I had had a gun in my hand, there certainly would have been another murder."34

The jury deliberated for just under an hour before returning a verdict of not guilty. Spracklin walked a second time. Outside the courtroom, the crowd besieged him with handshakes and good wishes. Asked what his future plans were, he replied, "I have no plans at the present time. I have nothing to say for publication. The future is before me but I have not decided what I will do."

---

34 *Toronto Daily Star*, February 24, 1921

CHAPTER 13

Although legally in the clear where Trumble's shooting was concerned, Spracklin lived under the threat of death for months afterward. When he was asked to attend a church service in London, Ontario, the pastor of the church in question received a note that read, "Don't let the murderer come here tonight. We will get him." Spracklin ignored the threat, and even turned up to play at a local hockey game. Spectators crowded the arena to get a look at the infamous pastor, who performed so well in the ice that he earned a standing ovation.

Encouraged, he went on to Paris, Ontario, where he preached a pro-temperance sermon at the town's Methodist church. Spracklin told his spellbound audience that a Toronto group calling itself the 'Determination League' had sent death threats to his home and warned him that if he set foot in that city on 'dry' business, he would be shot.

"I intend to disregard that message entirely," he declared while his listeners applauded. "I put one Sandwich roadhouse out of $10,000 a month. Is it any wonder I had to go through the tragedy of killing a man?"35

On February 27th, Spracklin appeared at the Divine Methodist church in Sarnia. He was introduced by the Reverend Dr. Samuel Chown, general superintendent of the Methodist church in Canada, who likened him to the Korean protesters punished by Japanese military authorities because it was "wrong to denounce."

"If it is wrong to denounce wrong, then Reverend J.O.L. Spracklin was wrong in denouncing the insidious things he saw with his own eyes," Chown told the assembly of over two thousand.

"Hear, hear!" the audience shouted.

"I know very well," Dr. Chown continued, "that those who think the liquor trade ought to

---

35 *Toronto World*, March 14, 1921

be handled with kid gloves think that he has gone too far. There are others of us who, knowing what a maelstrom of deviousness it is, know that there can't be a too far."

Then he introduced Spracklin who, as the paper put it, "figuratively raised the fiery cross of Methodism against the liquor forces in preparation for the Ontario referendum on April 18."36

"I thank God for the wonderful privileges He gave me in that work I have been engaged in during the last eight or nine months," the Fighting Parson said. "I thank God that He ever saw fit to call me to the task of which I did not know the extent when I started in, and I say tonight that although we did not perhaps accomplish all, still a great deal has been done for the good of the kingdom."

Over two thousand people listened as he urged, "I ask you for your prayers, for I am not yet through with the fight."

But he was- in Canada, at least. In late 1921 some women in his congregation, who may

---

36 *Toronto Daily Star*, February 28, 1921

have been agents of his local enemies, accused him of sexual improprieties. Myrle Spracklin and the Border Cities Ministerial Association stood behind him and the charges were never substantiated, but the Fighting Parson was emotionally exhausted from the string of courtroom battles. He left Canada in 1922 to take over a charge at Cheboygan, Michigan. While in the U.S., Spracklin became a vocal supporter of the Anti-Saloon League, appearing at its rallies and events as a public speaker. He served at one Michigan church after another (Homer, Davisburg, Bay City, Clio, Oscoda) and finally died in Greenbush, MI, on May 28, 1960.

Epilogue

The brief but spectacular career of the Reverend Leslie Spracklin can be likened in some ways to that of Eliot Ness, the dynamic federal agent whose relentless attacks on Al Capone's breweries and liquor supply routes played a role in the infamous Chicago mobster's downfall. Both men were young, unflinching in the face of danger, and resisted all efforts to buy or scare them off. Ness has endured in popular consciousness because the gangster he helped to take down –Al Capone- was an international celebrity. He also actively supported the publicizing of his feats, feeding one story after another to an eager press and even co-authoring an autobiography that was later adapted for a 1950s television series. Spracklin, on the other hand, resisted all post-1921 attempts to immortalize his Fighting Parson days in book or movie form, so once his story was no longer front-page news, the public quickly forgot him.

Ness supported the Prohibition laws because it was his job- Spracklin, as a Methodist pastor, had a moral hatred of the liquor traffic and suppressed it more out of a sense of duty than anything else. He was not bent on personal gain, and like all men who act from selfless motives, he did not court the publicity machine well enough to be remembered after Prohibition in the border cities was over.

BIBLIOGRAPHY

NEWSPAPERS

Border Cities Star

Detroit Daily News

Detroit Free Press

New York Times

New York Daily News

Pittsburgh Press

Toronto Daily Star

Toronto World

Windsor Daily Star

Woodstock Sentinel-Review

BOOKS

Barron, F. L. "The American origins of the Temperance Movement in Ontario," Canadian Review of American Studies, 1980

Butts, Ed. Outlaws of the Lakes: Bootlegging and Smuggling. Lynx Images Inc., 2004

Fraser, Chad. Lake Erie Stories: Struggle and Survival on a Freshwater Ocean. Dundurn Press, 2008

Gervais, C.H. The Rumrunners: a Prohibition Scrapbook. Firefly Books, 1984

Hunt, C.W. Booze, Boats, and Billions: Smuggling Liquid Gold. McClelland & Stewart, 1988

Jones, Bob. Cornbread and Caviar: Reminiscences and Reflections. Bob Jones University Press, 1985

Krasnick Warsh, Cheryl Lynn, ed. Drink in Canada: Historical Essays. McGill- Queen's University Press, 1993

READY FOR MORE?

We hope you enjoyed reading this series. If you are ready to read similar stories, check out other books in the *Organized Crime* series:

Bessie Perri: Queen of the Bootleggers
Rocco Perri was the Al Capone of Canada. Without him, the American market of alcohol would be a little...dry.

Rocco is frequently cited as the most successful bootlegger of Canada, however, for one important reason: his wife, Bessie Perri. If Rocco was the King of Bootlegging, Bessie was the obvious queen.

With page-turning suspense, this gritty book looks at the brains behind Canadian bootlegging and how her cutthroat ways forever changed the landscape of both prohibitions.

Bloody Valentine: The Bloody History of the Saint Valentine's Day Massacre

The Saint Valentine's Day Massacre is one of the most notorious murders of all time.

In the crime-ridden Chicago of the Prohibition era, gangsters like Al Capone battled for power, but few went to the extreme lengths that Capone did on that fateful day in 1929.

This short book gives you an exciting look at one of the most notorious criminals of all time, and the massacre he masterminded to finally gain control of the bootleg liquor trade.

Pray he has chocolates in that box and not a Tommy gun! This is one Valentine's Day you will never forget.

Public Enemy #1: The Biography of Alvin Karpis--America's First Public Enemy
Before John Dillinger, Pretty Boy Floyd, and Baby Face Nelson made the term "Public Enemy" famous, there was Alvin Karpis--one of the ruthless leaders of the Barker-Karpis gang.

It was him that J. Edgar Hoover first thought worthy of the title Public Enemy

In a page-turning style, this true crime book traces his criminal orgins from his young days as a bootlegger to his ultimate demise.

The Real Gangs of New York

The subject of a classic history by Herbert Asbury and an Academy Award nominated film by Martin Scorsese, the gangs of The Five Points in New York have become the stuff of legend. But how much is legend and how much is fact?

In this short book we examine the original gangs of the Five Points in New York and see how accurate the film was (spoiler alert: not very) and what Asbury may have gotten wrong in his original research on this era.

From the Bowery Boys to the Dead Rabbits, we look at the gangs that operated not just in the Five Points, but also those who wanted a piece of the action there and engaged in gang wars that would leave even modern thugs quivering in their boots!

Sam the Cigar: A Biography of Sam Giancana

Sam Giancana is one of the most famous gangsters in U.S. history, with rumored links to the CIA and President Kennedy.

But was he really involved in the assassination attempt on Fidel Castro and the assassination of J.F.K.?

This thrilling bio gives you all the details on one of America's most fascinating underworld figures.

The Maple Syrup Mafia: A History of Organized Crime In Canada

It's no secret that organized crime is everywhere. From Japan and Italy to Israel and Mexico, there seems to be no place on earth where an organized crime family doesn't exist.

You may think that one of the few safe places left is friendly, welcoming Canada, which many believe is so safe that people there always leave their doors unlocked. Think again.

This book delves into the often ignored but nevertheless bloody world of Canadian mobs. You'll meet the Rizzutos, a powerful family with connections to the legendary Five Families of the American Mafia. Then there's the Cotroni family formed by Vic "the Egg" Cotroni, an ex-wrestler with ties to the Ndrangheta.

You'll also learn about their connections to the blood-soaked Quebec Biker War, where the Hell's Angels and the Rock Machine battled for 17 years and claimed 150 lives. And just wait until you get to Toronto!

Prepare to be shocked by the true story of organized crime in Canada. It proves that there is truth to the expression, "it's the quiet ones you have to watch."

NEWSLETTER OFFER

Don't forget to sign up for your newsletter to grab your free book:

http://www.absolutecrime.com/newsletter